Scott Alexander
10-83

RHINOCEROTIC RELATIVITY

RHINOCEROTIC RELATIVITY

by Scott Alexander

Illustrations by Laurie Smallwood

Published by:
    The Rhino's Press, Inc.
    P.O. Box 2413
    Laguna Hills, Ca. 92653
    Ph. (714) 997-3217

Copyright © 1983 by Scott Robert Alexander
First Printing – July, 1983
Second Printing – August, 1983

Printed in the United Jungles of America
Library of Congress Catalog Card Number:
    83-060933
ISBN: 0-937382-02-7

CONTENTS

ACKNOWLEDGMENTS

I would like to thank the following people:

1. Anyone with a horn on the front of their head.
2. Everyone weighing over 5,000 lbs.
3. Anybody with two-inch-thick skin.
4. Everybody who pays money for this book.

DEDICATION

This book is dedicated to J & N, who are in the business of changing lives.

INTRODUCTION

Without a doubt, the most difficult part of writing a book is the starting of it. Early this evening, I sat down with some crisp, new, notebook paper. I poised my pen for action, and prepared to whip out the first couple chapters.

Hmmm . . . Writing the first line is extremely important, you know. It has got to be just right. Otherwise, the book may sit for months on the bookstore shelves unsold, because the first line failed to grab the potential reader's interest. Realizing the significance that my first thoughts may have on the marketability of my next literary work, I clicked my pen ready for action and proceeded . . . to think . . . carefully.

Yikes! If the beginning doesn't click just right, the book may never see an invoice with its name on it! If the first paragraph bombs, the rest of the book could be World War III! If the first line isn't just oozing with literary excellence, I may end up with a garage full of unsold books. On the other hand, if I can't write the first line, there ain't gonna be any book!

GET STARTED NOW!

Haha! I did it! I tricked myself into starting! Not only am I past the first line, but I am now going on to the second page! This isn't specifically meant to be a motivational book, but there is definitely a success principle illustrated here. It's a bonus thrown in . . . kind of like finding a parking space right up front.

That bonus is: if you will *just get started,* you can accomplish anything that you want to! It's true, and this book is proof before your very eyes. I've been thinking about writing this book for months! I never got started, and you never read the book, right? Until now!

I wrote the first sentence, then I went on to the second sentence, and here I am 22 sentences later! I guarantee you that there is an ending to this book, because now that I have gotten started, finishing it will be easy! Just reach around with your right forefinger to see if there is a back cover on this book. Yep, it's finished!

Chapter 1

REJECT MEDIOCRITY

Do you know the secret of how to be in control of your own life? Do you know what the secret of being financially wealthy is? Do you know the secret of being happy? Here it is. The secret is: *don't do what everybody else is doing!*

DON'T SUPPORT SLAVERY

Look around you. How many people can wake up in the morning and do whatever they want to do for the day? Hardly anyone, right? Of course, the reason is because they have to go to work. The trouble with that is that WORK IS A DRAG! But, being an economic blister is even more of a drag, right?

So, in order to avoid being broke, most people set off each day to a place called "work."

"Don't become a wage slave!"

MS. BEAUVINE

Can you imagine that? They not only have to show up *every* day of the week, but they are told how much money they will make, and when to plan their two week escape. They have, in effect, become "wage slaves," and their lives are no longer theirs. Why do people do that?

Certainly, it is not for financial gratification. How many millionaires do you know who became rich from their jobs? How many people do you know who became rich, period? Again, *most* people (95%) never get to the point where they do not have to worry about money. What an absolute shame to work from 20 to 50 years and never get ahead financially! Most people can barely pay their rent, let alone consider buying a plane, a yacht, or their own island in the Bahamas.

BUDGETS ARE GROSS

I know some people who even have budgets! How sickening! Can you imagine a life of such predictability that you know exactly how much you are going to spend for the month on gasoline and toiletries? Snap out of it! How are you ever going to get ahead if you *plan* on mediocrity?

Surely, there has got to be more to life than going to work each day in order to make the Volkswagen payment at the end of the month.

What about happiness? Well, how many people do you know who seem to be really happy?

Most people believe that happiness is only possible on the weekends! It's the T.G.I.F. syndrome! Saturday and Sunday are the two days that people escape and experience a little bit of freedom. Unfortunately, Saturday zips by, and on Sunday night they're bummed again because it's back to the big "W" tomorrow for another week.

WOULD YOU BE SATISFIED WITH A HAPPY HOUR?

Everyone wants happiness, but they cannot find it in how they are spending their lives, so they look for a substitute. Why do you think so many people drink so much alcohol? No one can be that thirsty! Why are so many people hooked on drugs? How come there are so many divorces? Certainly, these cannot be the signs of happy people! Some people are so unhappy that they just kill themselves. Most people are not that desperate though, so they just comotose themselves in front of the TV every night.

Wow! I have got to change the subject, because I am starting to get depressed! The point is that this is the way that most people live, and if you live like *most* people, you are going to be working all your life, broke and unhappy. If you follow the herd, you will become a cow just like all the others.

BE DIFFERENT

The secret is *don't do what everyone else is doing.* We know that most people are like cows, right? The individual who is financially secure, in charge of his life, and happy is definitely uncommon. They are a rare breed, but they are around. They are rhinoceroses!

The rhinos of the world are the thick-skinned chargers who enjoy the excitement of running in the jungle rather than following the herd to the meat market. By nature, rhinos buck the odds. They are willing to put themselves up against challenges, and the taunting and criticism that taking a challenge brings, to avoid mediocrity. They are eager to struggle upstream, in order to escape a commonplace existence that the cows all share. They are ready to risk losing, in order that they might win.

The theme of this book is rejection. To be successful, you have to reject the ways of the cows. You have to refuse to do what everyone else is doing. It's like buying stock. If you are buying the stock that everyone else is buying, you are probably buying the wrong stock. Also, if you are living the same way that everyone else is living, you are probably headed for an ordinary, uneventful, boring life, if you haven't already reached it.

HAPPINESS CAN MAKE YOU HAPPY!

You want success! You want meaning in your life and most of all, you want happiness, because what is the use of living if you can't be happy?

Happiness is a weird subject. Just as everyone has a different idea of what "success" is, so people have varying concepts of what "happiness" is. Most people have the idea that to be happy means to be content. To be content sounds appealing to only one type of person—a cow! A cow's major aim in life is to be content. Have you ever seen a restless cow? No, because if he was discontent, he would be a rhino!

That is the major difference between cows and rhinos. Cows prefer to lay around in pastures being content, while rhinos would rather be out in the jungles changing the world. Webster's defines "content" this way: "to limit oneself in requirements, desires, or action." Sound like anyone you know? Hopefully, not yourself!

If you are not content with your life, rejoice! If you cannot accept mediocrity, delight in the fact that you are not a cow! If there is any dissatisfaction in what you have accomplished so far, you have my deepest respect. Be fabulously happy that you are not content, and pray that you never find yourself in that disgusting state. Thank God that He gave you the energy to change the world!

What good is a content, old cow going to do anyone? How much inspiration are we going to draw from someone wasting away in a pasture, chewing his cud? COME ON!!! If you are not part of the solution, then you are a part of the problem! The world is in trouble, and if you are too lazy to get off your fanny, then you are causing the trouble!

LOOKING FOR A FEW GOOD HORNS

If you are not a charging, two-inch-thick skinned rhinoceros, then you are a wimpy, shiftless, impotent cow! Unless you put the horns on the *front* of your head and start acting alive, you are liable to be ignored, forgotten and lost!

Hey! I can't help but put the screw to you, because I am recruiting rhinos! Either you've got it or you don't! We are picking teams now, and you have got to decide whose team you want to play on.

The cow team is for the path of least resistance. They wait, watch, and procrastinate. We are the rhino team, made up of the fighters and the overcomers. Rhinos are for happiness, achievement, meaning, and leading the rest of the world. Either lead, follow, or shut up and get out of the way!

"The secret of success is to do the opposite of what everybody else is doing."

Chapter 2

THE ACHIEVEMENT ETHIC

I assume that if you have read this far, you have got to be a rhino! You want happiness, you desire success, and you plan on being in control of your own life. How? By doing the opposite of what most everyone else is doing!

Hey! This can be great fun, if you do it consistently. Of course, it takes guts and thick skin, because you will definitely stand out! You will be exposed to lots of criticism as the cows try to pull you down with them. Just remember that when cows disapprove, you are on the right track!

First, let's charge down success. Success can mean a lot of different things to different people, so let's start with "financial success." That means that you have to make money!

Sounds simple enough, but right off the bat, cows go about it the wrong way. They try to *earn* money, rather than *make* money.

COWS WORSHIP MONEY

Now, don't let the cows fool you. They may say that they have no interest in making money, but that is a rationalization to try to excuse their lack. Of course, money will not get you into heaven, but down here it is hard to go anywhere without it!

Cows will say that they do not want to make money their god. The irony is that sometimes it is those with the least amount of money who worship it the most. They complain that if only they had enough money, they could rid themselves of all their problems.

If you think that money will solve your problems, you are going to be a frustrated millionaire. Money will not wipe away all of your problems. You will just have *different* problems. If you are overcome with your problems, you need to work on the spiritual side of your life, which we will cover later.

Money is merely a tool to make your life more interesting. Naturally, when you have more money, you are going to have more options open to you. You can live a more creative, exciting, and satisfying life. That's what being a rhino is all about!

SUCCESS IS GIVING OUT
DEAD TURKEYS!

O.K. What is the first step? Well, the first step is to take a look at what the cows are doing, and then do just the opposite. Most cows work at a job all their lives, and never really get anywhere. Again, how many people do you know who became rich working at a job? There is only one practical way, besides investments, to become wealthy, and that is to have your own business.

Your chances of becoming rich at your job are extremely poor, I think you will agree. I don't suggest that you quit your job tomorrow, but I am recommending that you *plan* on quitting as soon as possible. The longer that you work for someone else, the longer you put off your chances for financial success.

The work ethic is dead! Going to college to get a good job is quickly becoming obsolete! Perhaps that was success in the sixties and the seventies, but we are in the eighties now! The *achievement ethic* is the code for today!

Success in the eighties is not having spent forty years of your life working for some big corporation, and then retiring with a dead turkey or a gold watch. Success, today, is creating your *own* corporation, and then giving out the dead turkeys and gold watches! The achievement ethic recognizes accomplishments, and pays for results, not effort.

WHAT ARE YOU WAITING FOR?

Plan on being in business for yourself as soon as you can. It doesn't matter what you do—JUST DO IT!! Don't wait until you get your MBA degree. That will only slow you down! If the professor knew anything about business, he wouldn't be teaching it....he would be *doing* it! Don't wait until you have more time, more money, or more energy. If you wait for any of that, you will wait forever! You have to do it now, or else you are just fooling yourself that you will ever do it.

There is presently a resurgence of interest in our free enterprise system, even though socialistic influences continue to pockmark the country like a cancerous growth. It is up to us rhinos to save free enterprise! If the free enterprise system were to ever disappear, all the rhinos would go with it. So be prepared to fight for what you believe in, or else start learning how to chew cud.

UDDERSTANDING COWLECTIVISM

Probably the biggest factor in our slide towards increasing socialism is the cow population amongst us. More specifically, it is the cow's ignorance and apathetic attitudes towards capitalism that are slowly eroding our freedoms. The system which made our country the greatest and the most free nation of the world is being raped right before our eyes!

Yet, who is responding? Certainly not the cows! They mistakenly believe that socialism would benefit them, while capitalism only benefits the rich. This attitude is due to two basic flaws in cows called "laziness" and "envy."

Cows do not believe in the achievement ethic, for a number of reasons. First, they just do not *want* to achieve. They like to lay around, chew their cud, and complain. Cows are not into expending energy, but enjoy being idle and dronish. Socialism sounds like their cup of tea, because the idea of having someone else support them is very appealing. Cows, by nature, are always looking for a handout. It doesn't matter whose hand it is, or what's in it. If it is free, a cow will take it, which leads us to the dangerous "free lunch" cow attitude.

FREEDOM IS THE PRICE THAT WE PAY

Rhinos understand that there is no free lunch. Cows cannot accept that fact and, therefore, are infected with the "something for nothing" complex. This is not an inborn peculiarity. Expecting something for nothing is an attitude that has been propogated by the supercows in Supercow City . . . Washington, D.C.

Supercows there implement free schooling, free school lunches, free public transportation, free food and shelter, free medical treatment, free money, and if there is anything else that you want for free, I am sure that they can get it for you! No wonder the "free lunch" disease is so prevalent!

There is definitely a price being paid though. Tragically, the price is more valuable than money. We are paying the price with our most precious commodity—*freedom.* When the government gives, the government has to take. Taking involves force, and whenever force is employed, somebody will come under the control of somebody else. Say goodbye to freedom.

If our freedom is being sapped, why do free lunch programs continue? The answer lies in the fact that there are more cows than rhinos, and the government bureaucrats respond to numbers, not common sense. It is a vicious cycle: the more they give, the more the cows demand. It's like helping an alcoholic by giving him a shot of whiskey every time he wants a drink!

THE PUSHER MAN

Understandably, the supercow bureaucrats certainly do not want to break anyone's bad habits. Their security is dependent upon everyone screaming for more. That is how they build big departments of bureaucracy. They request larger sums of money each year to redistribute, and they look for more people to "help."

Look at the government's poverty programs. Despite the billions of dollars that have been given away, we still have just as many poor people. The only difference is that poor people of today are *really* poor, because they have been stripped of their pride and initiative to help themselves. Chalk up another one for the pusher man.

What our country needs right now is to go cold turkey, before we are a dead turkey! John Hospers chillingly describes the consequences of our current redistribution-of-the-wealth philosophy:

> ". . . when it is no longer worth the producer's while to produce, when they are taxed so highly to keep the politicians and their friends on the public payroll that they themselves no longer have a reasonable chance of success in any economic enterprise, then of course production grinds to a halt . . . When this happens, when the producers can no longer sustain on their backs the increasing load of the parasites, then the activities of the parasites must stop also, but usually not before they have brought down the entire social structure which the producer's activities have created. When the organism dies, the parasite necessarily dies too,

but not until the organism has paid for the presence of the parasite with its life. It is in just this way that the major civilizations of the world have collapsed."[1]

If the trend of the last few decades continues, the jungles of America are liable to dry up, and the producing rhino is going to become extinct. In order to reverse the trend, we have to do the opposite of what everyone else is doing, and refuse to accept government favors, handouts, or benefits of any kind. It has to start somewhere, and it is very unlikely that it will start with the cows. Support America by supporting yourself!

Let others know how you feel, especially the cows! Cows really aren't that bad, they are just misguided. No one in college ever told them about this "no free lunch" stuff. In fact, it was encouraged there, with government student loans, financial aid programs, and socialist professors, which brings me to another point: If you feel like you *have* to go to college; learn all you can, but do not let them "educate" you!

BAKE YOUR OWN PIE

A second reason that cows would prefer socialism is just pure, unadulterated envy. If

1. John Hospers, "The Two Classes: Producers and Parasites," Reason (September 1975), p. 13.

they don't have the energy to achieve material wealth, they do not want to see anyone else achieve it either. That is sad.

With some cows, it is not envy so much as it is a misunderstanding of how wealth is created. One of the most destructive myths perpetuated by cows is the "pie theory." They picture all of the wealth and goods in a pie shape, and when someone takes a slice of that pie, there is that much less for everyone else. Well, that is typical cow thinking!

The rich do not get wealthy at the poor's expense. Quite the opposite is actually what happens. There is no fixed pie of wealth, goods, or services. You create your own pie . . . and then everyone comes running to get a slice of yours!

But you have to *create* it first! The more ambitious producers there are, the more charging rhinos there are, the more pies of wealth are created, and the more everyone benefits. Not *being* one of the poor is really the best way to help them!

PUBLIC ENEMY NO. 1

The next cow attitude to reject with a passion is that the world owes you a living. Nobody owes you anything! You owe yourself! I recently read of a welfare recipient who wrote to her welfare office and demanded, "This is my sixth kid. What are you going to do about it?"

You see, our biggest enemy is amongst us. Our freedom is not threatened by the communists, or aliens from outer space, nearly as much as it is by the cows that reside here. Actually, a "leech" much more accurately describes this type of menace. Remember, an animal can only support so many parasites before that animal weakens and dies.

Until everyone accepts the duty of solving their own problems, our freedom will continue to disappear, because socialism thrives on the shirking of responsibility. As long as people continue to blame their problems on society, and have no spirit of initiative or self-accountability, we are headed towards living under the control of supercows.

THE LUST TO CONTROL LIVES

In order to understand supercows, we first have to look at a couple basic traits of bovine behavior. One, which we have just discussed is the "pass the buck" syndrome. This is exhibited in those cows who lack the drive and leadership to look to themselves to solve their own problems. A complete lack of self-reliance is the reason cows like this demand solutions from others for their problems.

Unfortunately, there are those who love to help the cows. They are the bureaucratic supercows, and their motivation is an insatiable lust for power. I don't mean physical power or financial power, but power over others.

When you combine the supercow's desire to control lives and a cow's desire to be controlled, you have the perfect environment for socialism to thrive in. However, the main problem is *not* the supercows. They are a *result,* not a *cause,* of the real problem. Before we can rid ourselves of the regulating, bureaucratic supercow, we have to change a lot of cow's attitudes. As long as there are cows demanding quick, convenient, short-term solutions from others for their problems, supercows will continue to multiply.

BURIED IN THE NAME OF THE LAW

One of the supercow's tricks to temporarily patch up problems in society is to "pass a law." Passing laws has become an epidemic in this country. Each new law accumulates more force and power in government, which means less freedom for everyone.

New laws mean additional taxes to pay for its administration, more supercows needed to regulate what was once unregulated, new penalties for violating the new law, and higher taxes to pay for seeing that the new laws are not broken.

NO NOOSE IS GOOD NOOSE

Our government now has a noose around everyone's neck, and each new law and regulation that is enacted tightens that noose a little tighter. Cows are not aware of this as much as rhinos because, typically, cows are not exercising their freedoms as much as rhinos. Cows do not generally attempt to start their own businesses or try to improve their lot in life. But wait until they do! Then *they* will feel the restraint of the noose around their necks!

If you have never attempted to start a small business of your own, let's run through an example to show you just how tight the noose can get. Let's assume that you have worked hard at a job for the last five years and that you have managed to save $30,000. You realize that you will never get ahead financially if you continue working the rest of your life, so you want to put your money down on a limousine, and start your own limousine service.

Fantastic! By investing your savings in the limousine, you have created jobs at the car manufacturer, you have helped the car dealer make a profit which keeps everyone working there, and you are going to provide a valuable service to your community, besides giving part time work to your first driver. By taking the initiative to try to improve your life, you are going to create a stronger America . . . if you ever get things on the road.

A CHANCE TO MEET SOME UNCIVIL SERVANTS

First of all, you have to secure a license to operate a business in your city. The business license departments do not perform any public service. They are operated only as tax-collecting bureaus, and may possibly even demand a percentage of your gross sales, in addition to the license fee. Why do they need the money? So that they can pay the super-cows who are coordinating this big hold-up!

Next, go to the building and zoning department and check with them. Do not tell them that you are going to work out of your house, or you will not be in the limousine business for long. These are the supercows responsible for checking out your business location, and you just can't operate wherever *you* decide. They will decide that for you. You have to be in an area that is zoned for your type of business. Why do we have zoning laws? So that the zoning planners have something to do to earn your tax money, you big dummy!

THE EXCITEMENT CONTINUES

A limousine service, huh? Well, you need a limousine service license then! Don't ask why,

"Each new law and regulation tightens the noose a little tighter."

just get one . . . if you can. If you are located in Chicago, the chances are that you are already out of business, because they only decided to issue a certain number of licenses and they are all out. Oh well, maybe you can move to California!

When you get to California, stop by the Public Utilities Commission, get in line, and try to get a license from them. Depending on the mood of the cow at the counter, you might get lucky. You never realized that starting your own business could be this much fun, did you? Can you feel the noose tightening up?

Depending on how tight the noose is in your area, you may or may not be told how much you can charge a customer, but you *will* be told *how* you may charge. They will either allow you to charge by the time of use, by the mileage, or a combination of both, depending on how they feel that day, I guess.

DON'T HOOK UP THE PHONES YET!

Your application fee for the license will cost you about $100, but remember that this is only an *application!* They have not given you their permission to start the business yet! They may just decide to send you back to the old job as a content cow, telling you that capitalism is evil.

Meanwhile, they are going to check you out while you wait the four to ten weeks to see if you are permitted a license. You will have to sign a form that allows the supercows to check out your financial history through the criminal identification bureau, to determine if you are fit to run this business. It doesn't matter if your mom and dad support you. It doesn't matter how confident you are about your new business idea. Big Brother Supercow will have the deciding vote!

TAXES PAY THE BABYSITTER

If you get a license, there are just a few other details to take care of before you get started. First of all, depending on which state you are in, you may have to have the limousine checked out by the Highway Patrol. The purpose of this inspection is to assure that the limousine meets safety specifications which some supercow working for the state designed. By the way, your tax dollars paid him to do it. Good thing too, because you are obviously too stupid to realize that you need a safe limousine to attract customers!

Have you ever heard of the FCC? If you plan on installing a mobile telephone in your limousine, you will have to get a license from them. And depending on where you store your limousine, you may be required to get a permit from the fire department.

Periodically, they will drop by and inspect your place to make sure you are not touching hot stoves or sticking forks in the toaster. You thought that you had grown up, didn't you? Mommy and Daddy have just been replaced by the fire safety inspector, the zoning planners, the FCC, the Public Utilities Commission, and your local bureaucrat.

Are you still in the mood to try to get ahead? If so, GO FOR IT! Just be sure to keep accurate records of all the money you make, because the government wants their share for their babysitting fee. And if you don't pay them, they will throw you in jail! What do you think jails are for, anyway?

Here is a list of how you will pay for all their "help":

Federal
Income tax
Self-employment tax
Social security tax
Unemployment tax

State
Income tax – state of residence
Income tax – state in which business is located
Sales tax
Conservation tax
Retail sales license

County
Personal property business tax
Merchant's inventory tax
Merchant's license

City
Sales tax
Transportation tax
Business earnings tax
Business personal property tax

Is this free enterprise? Well, it is an adulterated version. I certainly do not believe that it is what America's founding fathers had in mind when they risked their lives signing the Declaration of Independence in 1776. They were throwing off the nooses that the British government had tyrannized them with. Their belief was in the freedom of the individual and what that individual could accomplish.

OBSCENE LOSSES

In a capitalistic, free-enterprise society, anyone with an idea and the guts to implement it, can start his or her own business. The motivation is, of course, to make a profit. Not an obscene profit! There is no such thing as an obscene profit! If you think there is, then you are a cow!

The "obscene profit" is another example of ignoramus cow thinking, which is threatening our country. If you make a profit, then you are a success, right? But if you make a large profit, then you are obscene? COME ON!!! Why don't the cows complain about large losses? Now that seems obscene!

Look at the postal system. Here is a service that the government has decided that only it can provide, and it continually loses money. Isn't that obscene? Our government was originally set up to protect the lives and property of all the citizens. How did they get into the business of delivering mail?

PAY EACH PLAYER $50

Certainly, you have heard of the word "monopoly." You probably thought it was something that the government tries to "protect" us from. Most people do not understand what a monopoly really is, because they went to schools which are government controlled. They are not going to teach anyone that the term "monopoly" originally meant: "an exclusive grant from the king to operate free from competition." In reality (we're talking real life), the government *creates* monopolies, it does not discourage them.

Do you know what does discourage monopolies? Free enterprise! Competition is the most efficient regulator, and there will always be competition when there is an absence of government regulation.

So what happens when the government makes competition illegal? Presto! You have a monopoly! Many large companies realize this and use it to their advantage to restrict competition. The truth is that a monopoly is almost impossible to obtain without the government's intervention.

FOR THE GIRL WHO HAS EVERYTHING

Understand that I do not want to overthrow the government. I realize that government is a necessary evil in the jungle that we live in. My only objective is to show that unnecessary government growth is eroding our freedoms.

Being big does not always mean being better. Government fits right into this category. It's like the boa constrictor that I bought Kim for her birthday a few years ago. What a neat pet . . . until it grew longer than we are!

Now it no longer has the charm that it used to. When it was only twelve inches long, we would reach into its aquarium with no fear of being eaten, and we would let it wrap itself around our necks. That's when it was small, and we were in control!

QUIT FEEDING THE GOVERNMENT!

Today, our boa constrictor is about seven feet long, and weighs about forty pounds. We no longer have the freedom (or desire) to reach

"Government, like snakes, can grow to the size where they become dangerous!"

into its cage unannounced or to play with it around our necks. The snake is now the master. If it doesn't want to come out of its cage, we change *our* plans!

I am guessing that we will never have our friendly, fun, little snake back again, because from what I have observed, snakes seem to keep growing rather than shrinking as long as they continue to be fed. Fortunately, governments can be trimmed to size. Unless, of course, they have already grown so large and powerful that we are afraid to mess with them. Then, like the snake, it is only a matter of time before it is big enough to eat you!

SUCH A DEAL!

Wow!! What a fantastic analogy! I knew that snake would be good for something someday! Actually, snakes do make interesting pets. They don't bark, they don't shed hair, you only feed them once or twice a month, there is no need for toilet training, and they don't take much room! I highly recommend one as a pet for you. In fact, if you're interested, we just happen to have one for sale! Have I got a deal for you!

Chapter 3

SAFARI SECRETS

In order to make your trek through the jungles of life more satisfying, there are a number of basic rules to follow. Number one is that you have to *cast off everything that is not absolutely necessary!* That sounds simple enough, doesn't it? But you would not believe all the excess baggage most people carry around their whole lives.

Again, I have to stress that *most* people carry these extra burdens. You are different! You are a very unique animal called a rhinoceros! Successful living is enough of a challenge without weighing yourself down with cow baggage. Get rid of everything that is going to slow you down; like a negative attitude, worrying, hatreds, unproductive habits, and most of all . . . unproductive friends. That sounds mean, but you cannot afford to be carrying any cows around on your back!

COWS KILL DREAMS

Don't worry about what your friends are going to think! If no one is talking behind your back, you are doing nothing with your life! If there are no cows secretly hoping that you will fail, then you have already failed! You never take the first step towards *real* success until you take your first step away from the herd! Do not worry about hurting a cow's feelings. They may seem to be on your side, they may seem to be sincere, but they are BAD NEWS!

A COW COMES TO VISIT

It's kind of like the guy who had a sick friend in the intensive care ward in the hospital. He decided to go visit him, so he put on his best coat and tie, and dropped in during visiting hours.

Well, his friend was in pretty bad shape. He had all the tubes going into his arms, and he couldn't speak because he was hooked up to an oxygen mask. But he had a nice color to his face and a twinkle in his eyes, so the visitor figured that his friend enjoyed his presence. He stepped next to his bed and just smiled.

After a minute or so, the visitor could see that his friend was starting to look very ill. The color had left his face, and his eyes became very dull. His friend couldn't speak because of the oxygen mask, but he frantically wrote out a quick note and passed it to the visitor.

Just as the sick man handed over the note, he passed away. The visitor threw the note into his coat pocket, and went running to find a nurse.

Three days later, the visitor was at his friend's funeral, wearing the same coat and tie. Reaching into his pocket, he found the note that his friend had scribbled out to him. He opened it and read, "You are standing on my oxygen tube!"

IF YOU HAVE COWS AS FRIENDS, YOU DON'T NEED ENEMIES!

Do not let the cows stand on your oxygen tube! Your essential oxygen is encouragement, possibility thinking, faith and hope. Cows will cut that right off, if you let them. You cannot afford to have even *one* cow for a friend.

All it takes is one drop of ink to discolor gallons of pure, fresh water. Just a pinch of strychnine is all it takes to kill you. One cow friend could be the one bullet that is capable of stopping you dead in your tracks! Don't risk it!

UNDERSTANDING SUCCESS

Rule number two is to *stay with the rhinos!*
Success is a challenging safari, and the more
rhinos that you know, the better. Success is
impossible to capture without the help and
cooperation of others. The more people that
you help, the bigger your success will be. If
you think about it, there is no successful person who did not in some way enrich or affect
the lives of others for the better. (Provided
what they did to get rich was legal!) There is
no way to be successful affecting only yourself.

In fact, the reason that most people are not
successful and the reason the U.S. is sliding
towards socialism, is because success is not
really understood. Success is *not* material
wealth, large bank accounts, monthly over-
seas vacations, or diamond rings. Those are
some of the *effects* of success!

Success is helping people get what they
want. That's it! Do you know what that means?
That means the more people you help, the
bigger your success! Do you know what else
that means? It also means that people who
do not have the effects of success have not
helped very many people!

What kind of a jungle do you want to live in—
a jungle where people are rewarded for im-
proving the lives of others, or a jungle where

helping others is frowned upon? That is the difference between capitalism and socialism.

RHINOS HAVE STAYING POWER

A third tip is that *when the chips are down, fortitude counts for more than anything.* You can be a success if you have nothing more than the guts to try! Sure, money would help. Obviously, the right contacts would be nice, or being in the right place at the right time might improve your chances. But the overriding question will always be: do you have the courage? The deciding factor will always be whether you have the spirit or not. If you have the endurance and the boldness, then *nothing* can stop you! Go do it!!

YOU NEED A COMPASS AND A LIGHT!

The fourth, and most important, rule is that in any uncharted jungle where there are no paths to point the way, one needs to rely upon a compass. Life is certainly an uncharted jungle, and though we have goals which lead us in certain directions, the underbrush can be very misleading at times. That's why, as important as the compass is to the explorer, so a safari guide is to you as you move into the unknown of each new day.

The original Safari Guide Manual explains, "In all thy ways acknowledge Him, and He shall direct thy paths." (Proverbs 3:6) Right there is your compass "directing your paths!"

He also says, "I have come as light into the world, that everyone who believes in Me may not remain in darkness." (John 12:46) There you have it—a combination compass and light!

But wait—there's more! "I am the bread of life; he who comes to Me shall not hunger, and he who believes in Me shall never thirst." (John 6:35)

The Bible also says "For God so loved the world, that He gave His only begotten Son, that whoever believes in Him should not perish, but have eternal life." (John 3:16)

God gave His Son for you! Hey, I am not making this up as I go along, you know! You can look it up yourself to double check!

Can you believe what a thrill it is to know Jesus Christ as your Safari Guide? *Nothing can go wrong!!!* He assures us "...God causes all things to work together for good to those who love God..." (Romans 8:28)

This is the secret of happiness! All you have to do is love God!

CHARGE TO THE NARROW GATE

Remember, the theme of this book is to do the opposite of what everyone else is doing, in order to find happiness. Here's how the Bible says it, "Enter by the narrow gate; for the gate is wide, and the way is broad that leads to destruction, and many are those who enter by it. For the gate is small, and the way is narrow that leads to life, and few are those who find it." (Matthew 7:13,14)

Whew! Thank the Lord that He led you to the narrow gate! I cannot understand what goes through the heads of those atheistic bovines! Atheists just don't have a prayer!

OPEN THE DOOR!

If you do not know Jesus Christ personally, I would recommend taking care of that immediately. There really is nothing more important, and what meaning could life possibly have without Him?

Jesus said, "Behold, I stand at the door and knock; if anyone hears My voice and opens the door, I will come in to him, and will dine with him, and he with Me." (Revelation 3:20)

You could have Him with you for dinner tonight if you ask Him into your heart right now. Here's a "request for Safari Guide" prayer to help you if you are at a loss for words:

"Dear Lord Jesus, I confess that I am a sinner. I believe that You are the Son of God, and that You died for my sins. I believe that You rose from the dead, so that I would be saved. Thank you, Lord. Now I want to open the door. Please come into my heart, fill me with Your

Holy Spirit, guide me, and take complete control of my life. Use me to Your glory, Lord, and I will serve You, as You give me strength throughout my life. In Jesus' name, I pray this. Amen."

YOUR FIRST ASSIGNMENT

Great! Now you can continue on your safari knowing that He will always be with you! The first thing you want to do is to get to know Jesus better. Being on a first name basis is not enough. You need to know Him really well, because He is now in charge of your safari!

God has written a long (we're talking lengthy!) letter to you entitled "The Holy Bible." The Bible may have seemed boring to you before, but that was before He was your Safari Guide. No wonder it was boring! That's like reading somebody else's mail! It is boring *no more,* because now it is written expressly for you!

For example, RIGHT NOW get your Bible and read 1 Thessalonians 5:18. Hurry, because I am not going to start again until you read what God has written to you there.

You thought I was kidding, didn't you? Well, what did it say? Are you going to do it? You *better* do it, because God is telling you right there that that is what He *wants* you to do!

It sounds like such a meaningless bit of advice, but just think what is going to happen to your attitude when you thank the Lord for everything. And He does mean *everything!!* When you break a horn off, or get hit by a torpedo, say "Thank you, Lord!"

Kim and I started doing this last year. At first, it was kind of an awkward, uncomfortable thing to do . . . just blurting out "Thank you, Lord!" At first, we did it in a joking fashion with each other, and soon it became a meaningful phrase that really brought us closer to the Lord. Soon, we advanced to doing it around friends, and then they started getting in on it.

GOD DOESN'T BREAK PROMISES!

When you are in heavy traffic, say it out loud, "Thank you, Lord!" When you wake up in the morning, say it before you brush your horns. When you eat your lunch, remember to thank Him. If you jog in the morning, tell him "thanks" between breaths. Do it *all* the time, no matter what the situation.

If you are hurt in an accident or develop cancer, say "Thank you, Lord!" and really mean it. Even though you can see no good in it, He *promised* that He would cause *everything* to work out for the best for those who love Him.

That is an actual promise made by God who created everything in the universe! And if He can make the universe in six days, He can surely keep a promise that He made to you! Just be sure to keep your part of the bargain, and "love the Lord your God with all your heart, and with all your soul, and with all your mind, and with all your strength." (Mark 12:30)

DON'T GIVE GOD
THE SILENT TREATMENT

After reading His word, the next logical thing to do is to talk to Him. I always appreciate hearing comments or questions about my book. I'm sure God loves to field questions about His book too! There is another fabulous promise in John 14:14, where Jesus says "If

" . . . and God created the rhinoceros."

you ask Me anything in My name, I will do it."
Wow! That could be anything from answering
your questions, to helping you start your own
business!

Learn to listen to God. He is probably not
going to communicate with you via the Goodyear blimp or throw lightning bolts at your
feet, so listen carefully. If you just talk, talk,
talk, and never listen, God probably doubts
your faith, or just figures that you are talking
to yourself.

A relationship with Jesus Christ is a lot like
making friends. First, you meet, and then every
time you get together after that, the friend-
ship becomes stronger and more meaningful. As you read His word, seek His guidance,
praise Him, and talk to Him, your relationship
will grow as you make the best friend that you
will ever have.

YOU HAVE GOT IT ALL

I am always curious about different people's
ideas of what life is all about. What possible
fun could life be for people who do not believe
in the Lord? What do they think is going to
happen to them when they die? What is the
use of their life? How horrible to think that all
you are is an evolutionary accident!

Christians, on the other hand, have everything! There are no monthly dues to pay, and

yet look at all the benefits you receive: salvation and a full-time Safari Guide to lead you through the jungle!

"For the eyes of the Lord move to and fro throughout the earth that He may strongly support those whose heart is completely His." (Chronicles 16:9)

What would you have going for you if you didn't have the Lord? A Rolls-Royce is neat, but it will never forgive your sins! An impressive title with a big company is O.K., but it will not "prosper you abundantly" like God can! And a Lear jet would be fun, but "those who wait upon the Lord will mount up with wings like eagles . . ."

Your whole concept of life changes when the Lord is in control, because you are going to look at everything differently. How close you are to the Lord is going to determine your attitude about life. It is going to affect how you react to difficult situations, and it is going to decide whether you live a life of joy, hope and faith, or a life of uncertainly, worry and death.

The secret of success and happiness (although we certainly do not want to keep it a secret) is to reject the wide gate that attracts all the cows, and *charge* through the narrow gate that leads to life! Thank you, Lord!!!

"Put on the whole armour of God" Eph. 6:11

Chapter 4

EVOLUTION IS NOT
THE SOLUTION

As you begin to read the Bible, remember that it is God's letter to you. Sure, the book was probably printed in some big, noisy factory in Los Angeles somewhere. True, God did not sit down one evening and actually put the words to paper Himself.

He used His secretaries! In fact, God used over 40 different people over a period of 1600 years to write the Bible! Most of these 40 people never knew each other, and were not even aware that anyone else was helping. God supervised the whole job!

"All Scripture is inspired by God . . ." (2 Timothy 3:16) It is important that you know that!

There are three specific ways that God reveals Himself to us. One way is through His

Son, Jesus Christ, who is now your Safari Guide.

DOESN'T SMELL FISHY TO ME

The second method He uses is the Bible. In it are the answers to everything! You have *got* to believe that! Belief in the Bible is the number one prerequisite for living a successful and happy life.

You have to believe it all! If you start questioning certain parts of the Bible, you are questioning God. It is *fun* to believe in the Bible! But you have to believe *every* word.

It amazes me that some people do not put complete faith in the Bible, because of stories like Johan being in the belly of the whale for three days. *Come on!!* If you can't believe that story, you sure don't have much faith! I've seen more unbelievable things on "That's Incredible!"

Jonah 1:17 says that "the Lord prepared a great fish to swallow Jonah, and that Jonah was in the fish for three days and three nights." Then Jonah prayed to the Lord asking forgiveness, and "the Lord commanded the fish, and it vomited Jonah up onto the dry land."

What is the problem? Would it be easier to believe if the Bible said that the Lord prepared a submarine to pick up Jonah, and after three days it returned him to the shore? Hey! If God chooses to prepare a great fish to swallow Jonah, then He can *prepare* a great fish!! That is a small order for God! Have a rhinoceros faith in God! You're a big thinker, aren't you? Don't let little, cow thinking get in your way!

YOUR PARENTS CAN'T DO IT

To live your life for happiness (not popularity), you have to establish the Bible as your Safari Guidebook, and then live by it. It is the truth. Question everything else that you hear or read, but never doubt your Safari Guidebook!

See, this way you have established God as the directing force in your life, not other people. Who else could possibly make you happy and successful, like God can? Do you think the government can? A lot of people (cows) do believe that, indicated by the dramatic growth of the federal bureaucracy.

Do you think your parents can make you happy and successful? Mom and Dad may be great people, but did they ever raise anyone from the dead? How about your college professor, then? Well, he may be able to explain the intricacies of the Big-Bang Theory, but did he ever tell you the story of David and Goliath?

When you establish the Word of God as your guide for successful living, it automatically helps you make decisions that will make you happier. For example, when you are in your college biology class and the teacher is discussing evolution, you can just tune him out, because you know that he is obviously misguided.

The Bible says that "In the beginning God created the heavens and the earth." (Genesis 1:1) You have decided to live by the Word of God, not the word of man, so there is not even a decision to be made, because you already made it. You're on God's side!!

THE WORLD'S GREATEST HOAX

Creation is another way in which God revealed Himself to mankind. Psalm 19:1 says, "The heavens are telling of the glory of God; And their expanse is declaring the work of His hands." Who are you going to believe . . . God, or your egghead teacher? (Did I slant that question?)

You certainly have the choice to believe in evolution, if you want to. But *why* would you want to? To me, it would seem to be more fun to razz the teacher, rather than sit there looking like a protozoan with an I.Q. of bean dip, accepting everything he says. Get your horns out, put on your two-inch-thick skin, and challenge that sucker!

EVOLUTION GETS OLD AFTER A WHILE

Understand that there are different theories of evolution. Two important points to note here are that it is all theory, not fact, and they can't even agree on which theory they want to run with. In fact, to fully comprehend how asinine the idea of evolution is, read a book on it! Evolution doesn't make sense, so the book won't either.

Basically, all the theories run along a few premises, one of which is that evolution has occurred over tremendously long periods of time. That is a cop out! Because evolutionists cannot prove anything today, they always refer to the "primeval past."

The truth is that long periods of time would only be a deterrent to evolution, because of a scientific principle called "entropy." Entropy is the tendency from the highly organized downward toward the less organized.

Gosh, I don't want to burst anyone's bubble, but as you become older, you tend to look older. After about 90 years, you are going to look like . . . well, you are going to look like you've been around for 90 years!! 900,000,000 more years certainly will not help your situation!

GOD DESERVED A DAY OFF

Another foundation of evolution is the belief that *mutations* caused the changes that resulted in the transition of one life form into another until—PRESTO!—here we are! This is really stretching it, don't you think? Talk about strong belief! Anyone who believes in evolution has to have far more faith than any Bible-believing Christian!

All a Christian has to believe is that God created the world in six days, and on the seventh day, He rested. Now that makes sense to me. You would probably want to rest on the seventh day also!

TODAY'S SALAMANDERS HAVE NO AMBITION!

Imagine a faith in which you believed that somehow the sun (Wait! How did the sun get here?) managed to hit a speck of slime at the right angle, and it transformed the slime into an amoeba. The amoeba promptly became a salamander, since it decided that having four legs would be easier to move around on.

Then the salamander had a mutation, which caused its kids to be born with eyelashes. They didn't have eyes yet, but they figured that the eyelashes would be useful for something! After three billion years, a pupil developed, but since the optic nerve had not arrived yet, the eyelash and the pupil had to wait another billion years.

Finally, the eye all came together, and the salamander could see that his future was in flying. He evolved a nice set of wings, grew a sharp beak, took flying lessons, and he turned into an eagle!

Now, his brother and sister salamanders had different ideas. Some evolved into elephants, some into chickens, some into people, and some were happy just being salamanders. And that explains why today there are still salamanders, and amoeba, and simple one-celled organisms . . . *they just have no ambition!*

ONE MILLION FRUIT FLIES CAN'T BE WRONG

You can believe that mutations are responsible for evolution, but pray that *your* kids are never born with one. T. Dobzhansky, in his book, "Genetics and the Origin of Species" states, "A majority of mutations, both those arising in laboratories and those stored in natural populations, produce deteriorations of the viability, hereditary diseases, and monstrosities. Such changes, it would seem, can hardly serve as evolutionary building blocks."

We could go on and on, but I suggest that you do some further research on your own. Actually, the more you learn about things like the fossil record, dinosaurs, DNA and mutations, the more your belief in the Bible will be strengthened.

"Evolution of the cow."

But you don't want to wear yourself out arguing with eggheads. I don't ask people *why* they believe in evolution. I want to know what they get out of believing in evolution! How could believing that life is just an accident make you happy? How could believing that you evolved from a monkey add much meaning to your life? How could believing that there is no purpose to life, add any purpose to *your* life?

DON'T WAIT TO EVOLVE INTO SUCCESS!

Life *does* have purpose and meaning, and life can be filled with happiness . . . if you reject the wide gate. Evolution has been widely taught and accepted because it rationalizes being miserable. Refuse to be involved in the greatest farce ever perpetrated.

Don't wait for time to make you better, go after your goals right now! Don't become a fossil yourself by waiting for the right time. *Now* is the time! Are you going to monkey around forever, or are you going to accomplish something? What are you waiting for . . . a mutation? CHARGE!!!

Chapter 5

GET RECKLESS

You crack the sunroof of your BMW just enough to let a little of the cool, night air brush across your face. It's beautiful out tonight, and you are feeling like the world is yours. As you gain speed, you appreciate the way your car handles the road. The wheels hug the road almost effortlessly. You're doing 60 m.p.h. now, yet you're in complete control.

You turn the radio on and hear your song. This is the song that motivates and inspires you. When you hear this song, you think of everything you are going to accomplish and what a fabulous life you are going to live.

Your body vibrates as you turn the volume up. You can actually feel the energy and power of the music, because your whole body is enveloped in it.

TWO-INCH-THICK GOOSEBUMPS

You step on the gas, and the car hits 75 m.p.h. As the cool wind whips through the sunroof, the air bites the back of your neck. Immediately, goosebumps march from your neck down to your kneecaps while the music continues to massage your body.

At top speed, you approach the corner. Just a little more volume and a little more open window. You can feel the goosebumps on your scalp now. Flat out, and you are in complete control as you effortlessly glide through the turn as if you are flying.

Whew! Have you ever done that? Isn't it fun? That is what success feels like! That is feeling great, and that is how you want to live your life! Take that music, the cool night air, the power and response of your car, and make that your attitude towards life! Take the goosebumps and make that your dream!

LIFE IN THE FAST LANE

One of the most successful men that I have ever met suggests that to succeed, you have to *"get reckless!"* Let's do it!!

Do you know that you and I can change the world? We're the ones that will do it too! There is no competition! No one else will dare go over the speed limit! Practically everyone is living for safety and security. Most people do not like to extend themselves financially, physically, or emotionally. You've heard the sayings, "Don't work too hard" and "Take it easy." That's what all the cows are telling each other!!

All we have to do is get reckless! What do you say? Are you game? The movers and the shakers are simply those who go over the limit. Get out of the traffic, and live your life in the fast lane! Turn up the music, throw down the top, and enjoy the wind in your face!

RECKLESS ASSOCIATES

Let's do this. We will all start living recklessly, change the world for the better, and then rendezvous in 1994 to swap stories! In fact, we could start a world famous "GET RECKLESS CLUB!" Membership would be limited to those who have demonstrated their recklessness by achieving what others said couldn't be done.

We could come up with our own sort of Nobel Peace Prize . . . maybe a "Reckless Rhino Reward"! Of course, there would be a secret "reckless" handshake, as we shout *"Get Reckless!"* to each other. Boy, I can see the story on this now in "The National Enquirer"—"NEW CULT RECKLESSLY SPREADING ACROSS U.S.!"

GOD IS A CHARTER MEMBER

Actually, I don't think that God would mind. He would probably be a big supporter of the whole thing! You can't get any more reckless than Jesus was while He was here on earth! Jesus didn't even have a BMW and He still managed to be quite reckless! His twelve disciples followed suit, and also lived in the same daring fashion. All twelve were persecuted for something that they believed in.

Wow! The more I think about it, the more I am blown away by the awesome recklessness of Jesus Christ. We complain about the high cost of renting office space, and yet Jesus got on with His business even though He never had a cent. We will abandon our plans when a relative calls us a "dreamer." Jesus was taunted unceasingly, beaten and whipped for His work, yet He persisted. We worry about getting door dings on our cars. Jesus had nails driven through His hands and feet to hold Him dying up on a cross between two thieves.

Just the thought of losing money can give us cold feet. Jesus gave His life!! More than that, He gave it knowingly and He could have gotten out of the whole thing by calling a legion of angels to rescue Him.

JESUS NEVER WATCHED T.V.

Imagine if Jesus did cow out! What if He had decided that it was just too much for Him, and bagged the whole deal? He could have decided to get a nice, safe job as a carpenter, put a little money in the bank, rent a cozy, little apartment, and spent His evenings watching T.V.!

But He didn't! His life and recklessness saved the world!

DON'T BE AFRAID OF FAILURE!

All you have to do to start living recklessly is to have a dream. You see, you are *already* over the speed limit, because very few people even have a dream. Why are people afraid to dream? For the same reason that they are afraid to attempt anything that is not required of them—*fear of failure!*

Part of living recklessly is to laugh at failure. Failure is merely a process of success. If you never fail, you will never succeed. Reckless living is not being concerned with pain or hurts. You are going to have them! Realize it now and be thankful for them, because they are going to thicken your skin so that you can get even more reckless!

To live a good, reckless life you also have to have no fear of death. Death is actually a step up! Death here in the jungle, means new life with Jesus Christ! The only death to fear is the death of your dream. If that dies, you automatically qualify as a cow!

WHAT IS YOUR DREAM?

Simply *having a dream* qualifies you as a Reckless Associate! But it has got to be a dream that gives you goosebumps! It has got to be a dream that puts you back in your BMW going 100 m.p.h. with the radio blasting! It has got to be something that makes your whole 6,000 pound body vibrate from horn to toe!

Quitting your job is not a big enough dream. Anyone can quit their job! (And I highly recommend it!) But how is that going to improve the world? A million dollars is not enough of a dream either.

Remember that money is the *effect* of a dream. If money is all that you want, your best bet is probably smuggling heroin! Or, if you want to get a lot of money and see the country, travel across the U.S. robbing convenience stores along the way. Extortion, kidnapping, forgery, and blackmail are also excellent ways of making big bucks fast.

See, money is not a good dream. How about building the world's most advanced hospital for cancer patients? Or how about starting a college that teaches free enterprise concepts and starts young people out on entrepreneurial careers? Have you ever thought about building a church bigger than Dr. Schuller's? Look at the impact that he has had on the world. Why not you?

You could do the same thing if only you had the dream! Most people do not even consider it though because they look at Schuller's Crystal Cathedral and think "I don't know where to get the money."

Hey! Schuller didn't start with everything that he has now. He started with basically *nothing,* and that may be where you are now! Desire is all it takes! And desire is free!! You can get as much of it as you want!

PRESIDENT RHINO

Just think. Whatever your dream is, it does not need money to be launched. All it takes is desire! Whatever you get an ambition for and an eagerness to work on will be yours. *Anything!!*

Do you want to be President of the United Jungles of America? Who says that it can't be you? Only you! Or would it excite you to be the leader of a marketing organization that involves tens of thousands of people all over the world? There are scores of people that have such businesses now. There are no prerequisites except for a burning desire. Do you have it? Can you *get* it?

"What is your dream?"

GOD HAS GIVEN YOU A CHALLENGE!

Mere wishing or a faint hope is not enough. Most people can't get a burning desire for a dream because their dream is not big enough to create goosebumps, or else they do not believe that they are capable of achieving that dream.

Well, here is a chance to check out your recklessness! God says that you CAN do it with His help (". . . with God all things are possible.") Matthew 19:26, and I challenge you to prove Him right!

Come on!! God is looking for people like you to achieve great things so that He will be glorified! Not many have the guts to take Him up on it! Do it and shock your neighbors!

Once you have your dream and you have run it by God for approval, nourish it. Dreams are very fragile and need extra care while they are still in the sprouting stages.

Keep in mind that the biggest dangers to a new dream are your relatives and friends (unless, of course, they are rhinos!). Your best bet is to keep your dreams to yourself and the Lord. When you spout off to everyone about what you are going to do, you let off steam and energy. Sometimes *talking* about dreams replaces *working* toward dreams! Don't let that happen to you!

SOMETHING TO THINK ABOUT

"We become what we think about." Isn't that an awesome thought? Did you know that you are today what you have been thinking about since you were a little rhino? In five years, you will become what you are thinking about today! Better be careful what you think about! In fact, if you are a cow, thinking can be very dangerous!!

Naturally, it would be advantageous to think about your dream. Put that in your thinking box! Instead of watching the Electronic Income Reducer (TV), imagine your dream in every detail. Before you go to sleep at night, plan your dream. Keep thinking about it constantly, and you will become your dream!

Finally, get reckless! This is *your* dream! No one is going to fight for it, unless you do! Adopt the attitude of "DO or DIE!" You're going to die eventually anyway, so it might as well be a meaningful death, right? Right! Charge recklessly!

It is not going to be easy, but not as difficult as living in mediocrity. You are going to hurt, but you will never know the pain of regret. You will encounter many difficulties, but remember that if you drive fast enough, the obstacles will become a race course! See you in 1994 at the "Get Reckless Club"!

"President of the United Jungles of America."

PRESIDENT RHINO

PRESIDENT OF THE UNITE

87

(Editor's note: Please keep in mind that this driving over the speed limit stuff is only an analogy used to convey a feeling. We don't want anyone dying in a fiery wreck after reading this chapter!)

Chapter 6

FAILING AIN'T THAT BAD

As you charge recklessly through the jungle, remember that the only way to succeed is to fail. That doesn't sound right, does it? Well, do you want to be rich or do you want to be right?

If you are ever going to find success, you have got to go out into the wild jungles and fail! You might have to fail a lot! You might have to fail so much that you feel like a failure!

Hey! Nothing could be further from the truth! Actually, the more you fail, the closer you are to success. Remember, everyone else is playing it safe and getting nowhere. Conformity guarantees failure!

WILL YOU KEEP TRYING?

Just keep charging and keep trying! Most of the world's millionaires never made it on their first attempts. Many failed for years and years until they captured success.

Thomas Edison tried over 1,000 different experiments until he found the right filament that would keep a lightbulb burning. Did he fail? Maybe it looked like failure after experiment number 512. It might have looked pretty grim after 850 experiments.

But after 1,000 attempts, it was success! Thomas Edison said that he didn't fail 1,000 times. He said that he only found 1,000 ways that it wouldn't work. What a rhino!

Naturally, you want to enjoy success the rest of your life. But are you willing to keep trying if things do not work out the first time? Are you prepared to try 1,000 times? Do you have the gumption to keep trying if it takes you thirty years?

Keep in mind also, that time is not the only element that you are fighting. If time were the only consideration, success would be easy. Probably the biggest obstacle to success is the suffocating mass of cattle that wanders the earth. Cows are innocuous looking animals, but they are capable of killing your ambition, draining your preserverance, and annihilating your dreams. Could you deal with them for thirty years?

INNOCULATE YOURSELF
AGAINST COWS

You *can* innoculate yourself against the sickness of the cows! There is an antidote that has been around ever since we were put on the earth. With it, you can ward off the negative effects of cow thinking, and eventually, you can develop a complete immunity to the sickness that cows spread. The antidote is *your own attitude.*

Attitude is just like snake venom. It can kill you almost instantly, or it can be used to save your life. It all depends on how you use it. The good news is that *you* get to choose how to use it! Nobody can decide for you whether to use your attitude positively or negatively. It is a freedom that can never be taken away. God gave it to you, so use it wisely!

Choose to have the right attitude, and you choose success. Isn't it funny that with all the different theories of success, all the books, all the speakers, and all the psychologists, all success really is, is a *choice!* And everyone has a choice! It is pathetic that most people live their lives tied up in chains, and never realize that their own attitude is the key that can turn them loose.

A ROLLS-ROYCE IS A CHOICE

Have you made the choice yet to be a success? Some people are afraid to commit themselves to anything without "thinking it over." Don't be so stupid! There is nothing to think over. Make your decision, and you are on your way! Let's settle this thing once and for all. Go get a pen and check the box that applies:

☐ Yes, I choose success!

☐ No thank you. I choose to be a failure.

Fantastic! Now we can get on with it! There are no more decisions to be made regarding your success. When you wake up in the morning, you do not have to wonder what the day is going to be like. You already know! Doesn't that make you feel warm and fuzzy inside? Ain't it great!

CAN RHINOS SWIM?

Now you can set off on your safari for success! To really make it a blast, there are a few attitudes worth developing. One is to remember that life is an adventure. You are going to be exploring the deepest forests, trekking across lonely deserts, discovering beautiful waterfalls, climbing mountains, crossing great rivers, and experiencing the thrills and dangers of the jungle.

Yes, of course you are going to come across some dangers. This is the real jungle you're playing in, not Disneyland! You are liable to have a crocodile bite off your leg. That could set you back a few days!

There is the chance of falling into quicksand, or tipping over in the canoe. The jungle is the home of disease-carrying bugs which can bite through two-inch-thick skin. There are lots of exciting, little perils hiding in the jungle just waiting to cause you all kinds of challenges!

SAFARI GUIDEBOOK PROMISE

But don't worry! God to the rescue!! See, I told you that you would appreciate having a good Safari Guide! Paul says in Phillipians 4:13, "I can do all things through Christ who strengthens me."

Fabulous! Now, whatever tricky situation or challenge you find yourself in, count on the Lord to strengthen you. Notice that Paul says "I can *do* all things through Christ..." He didn't say "I can *get out of* all things through Christ..."

Paul is not saying that Christ will *rid* you of your problems, but that He will *strengthen you,* so that you can get yourself out of the problems.

If you find yourself trapped in the quicksand, God will help you out, not by making the quicksand disappear, but by giving you the strength to get yourself out. Should you find

yourself in the river with the hungry crocodiles, the Lord will probably not shoot the
crocodiles for you. Instead, He will give you
the determination and energy and ideas necessary to take care of the situation yourself.

God knows what is best for you, and you
can continue on confidently, because you
know that He will never leave you, no matter
what happens! God personally guarantees
that in your Safari Guidebook. (Deuteronomy
31:8 Look it up yourself!)

Here's a thought to consider when your
safari through life gets rough, and you wonder if God has abandoned you in the deepest
part of the jungle:

"Many of us lose confidence in prayer
    Because we do not realize the answers.
We ask for strength, and God gives us
        difficulties
    Which make us strong.
We pray for wisdom, and God sends us
        problems
    The solution of which develops wisdom.
We plead for prosperity, and God gives us
    Brain and brawn to work.
We plead for courage, and God gives us
    dangers to overcome.
We ask for favors, and God gives us
    opportunities."

                                Author Unknown

MAKE IT HAPPEN!

Remember that you will never succeed if you never fail! You will never see the jungle if you don't see the quicksand! You will never feel the breeze at the top of the mountain if you don't feel the climb on the way up! You will never develop thick skin if you don't get hit a few times!

Go out *asking* for it!

"God will give you the courage to deal with the crocodiles!"

Chapter 7

JUNGLE MYTHS

To live an *imbalanced* life should be one of your long term objectives. See, you thought that you were supposed to live a well-rounded, balanced life, didn't you? Come on! That is a cow rationalization for never being good at anything! Being a well-rounded, homogenized, balanced individual is boring!

You have got to get unbalanced quickly! "Everything in moderation" is a fallacy that will keep you from rising to the top! There is an important aerodynamic law that says in order for a flying rhino to rise, *thrust must exceed drag!* Moderation just isn't going to do it! If you want to get anywhere in life, you are going to have to turn on your engines to develop some thrust!

In Revelation 3:16, Jesus says "So because you are lukewarm, and neither hot nor cold, I

"Those who wait upon the Lord will mount up with wings like eagles. . ." Is 40:31

will spit you out of my mouth." Be hot or cold, but never be in the bland, indifferent, and average stage between the two. Charge hot and hard!!

UNDRESS FOR SUCCESS

Another weird bit of advice floating through the jungle is the adage to "dress for success." This is the notion that the way to succeed on your safari is to wear a dark blue, pin-striped suit with a white shirt and a rep tie. (Whatever that is!) You know what I think of when I see someone dressed that way? *WORK!* I actually get a very uncomfortable, awful feeling inside of me when I see my blue, pin-striped suit hanging in my closet because it reminds me of when I used to have a job!

If you are already a millionaire, are you going to wear that garb that identifies you as someone trying to "dress for success?" Of course not! If you have already made it, then you don't need to impress anyone anymore! You can dress the way that you want to!

Dressing comfortably-rich will give you a more awesome posture! Instead of spending $300 on an executive suit, invest a little more and wear the clothes of the executive's employer! If you are dressed in obviously expensive casual clothing, you will present a more successful appearance than the guy in a three-piece business suit who looks like he's dressed to try to sell you something!

GOD WANTS YOU TO LOVE HIM

Our Safari Guide is also many times misunderstood. Oftentimes, God is presented only as the One who can bring you riches and success if you believe in Him. Prayer is portrayed as a "quick-fix" out of financial difficulties, and to be a Christian means that you stick the little fish symbol on the back of your new Cadillac.

God may help you become financially secure. On the other hand, maybe He will make it more difficult for you for some reason. Who knows! You can't go around second guessing God! You have just got to believe that *whatever* happens, God will cause it to work out for your good.

The point is that the Lord doesn't want you to come to Him because He is handing out free toasters or validating parking tickets. God wants you to come to Him because you *love* Him! Jesus Christ died for your sins! That should be your reason for loving Him!

JESUS OFFERED MORE THAN MONEY

While Jesus was here on earth, He didn't make anyone rich. That's not what He was offering. His offer was the chance to live forever with Him in God's Kingdom. His offer was one of joy and "the peace of God, which surpasses all comprehension." (Philippians 4:7)

Jesus did not come to earth promising to put everyone in the 50% tax bracket! He brought salvation and a peace that surpasses all human understanding. And when you are in the 50% tax bracket, you need a peace like that!

SUPPLEMENT YOUR HAPPINESS

Happiness is great, but it has one drawback, and that is that it is fleeting. Sometimes you've got it and sometimes you don't. Happiness comes and goes depending on your circumstances. When everything is going great, you are getting along with your spouse, there is extra money in the bank, the kids are doing good in school, and the weather is fantastic, you are happy.

But then the weather turns, your spouse dents the car fender, the kids are complaining, there is not enough money at the end of the month, and now you are depressed!

Nuts! If only that darn car loan was paid off! If only the wind wasn't blowing so hard! If only the carpet in our house wasn't so filthy dirty! See, it is always circumstances dictating your happiness.

Happiness is still great, but it needs to be supplemented with God's perfect peace. It's kind of like an insurance policy against depression. With Jesus Christ as your Safari Guide, your tires can all go flat, and the rain can come down in a torrent, but you will still have the joy of the Lord!

EXCHANGE YOUR CURRENCY

Since money is an external circumstance, having lots of it to take care of your needs brings a certain happiness. Money *can* buy happiness, but it *can't* buy God's perfect peace. They don't use money up there like we do down here. God really has no use for paper dollars, even silver certificates. Gold has no value to God other than to pave a street with it as if it were asphalt. (Revelation 21:21)

When Kim and I went to Australia, we brought over currency from the United Jungles of America which the Australian rhinos didn't want. Even the cows over there didn't want it! They all wanted *Australian* dollars!

In order to buy anything, we had to go to a bank and exchange our currency for theirs. Well, it is going to be the same situation when we leave here for God's Kingdom. Our currency has no value in Heaven! In fact, the customs men at the gate won't even let you bring it in!

STORE UP TREASURES

Plan ahead now! You know for a fact that you are going to Heaven sometime within the

"With Jesus Christ, your tires can all go flat, and the rain can come down in a torrent, but you will still have the joy of the Lord."

next dozen or so years, right? Then make plans to be rich in Heaven by exchanging as much of your currency as you can now into the currency that is used up there!

1 Timothy 6:17, 18 says "Instruct those who are rich in this present world to do good, to be rich in good works, to be generous and ready to share, storing up for themselves the treasure of a good foundation for the future, so that they may take hold of that which is life indeed."

Do you know what that means? It means that you can't take your money with you to Heaven, but you *can* exchange it for heavenly currency and store up treasures in Heaven!

BE A MILLIONAIRE TWICE

How do you exchange United Jungles of America dollar bills for currency that God will honor? Do what the Bible just said . . . "do good, be rich in good works, be generous and ready to share!"

Remember that the more money that you make here on earth, the more potential you have to do good! With lots of dollars, you have more to be generous with! A good long range goal would be to make a million dollars here on earth, and then exchange it into currency that will make you a millionaire in Heaven!

Of course, you don't want to wait until you have accumulated a million dollars. Your number might come up before then! Get started today with what you have now, and "take hold of that which is life indeed!"

"You can't take it with you, but you can exchange it for heavenly currency!"

Chapter 8

HOW SWEET IT IS

We had ants at our house a few months ago. You know how it happens—one hot day you're eating watermelon, and the next day there is a line of ants about three miles long that circles the perimeter of your house, runs along the inside roof and leads directly to the watermelon rind that you left sitting on the counter.

What are you supposed to do with the watermelon rind? If you throw it in the trash, the bag gets all wet, and you don't have time to chop it into small pieces and then stand there stuffing it down the garbage disposal.

Hey, you are a rhino! You've got things to do, people to see, goals to charge at! You can't be wasting your time trying to decimate a piece of watermelon rind! So you leave it on the counter.

WATERMELON RADAR

Usually, you discover the ants the next morning. Just after you go to bed, they turn on their watermelon radar and then they organize their march. How do those tiny ants with their tiny, little brains know to do it at night when we're all asleep?

Isn't that amazing? Did you know that with all that man has been able to create, no one has ever been able to make an ant! Isn't that crazy? Look at all the space-age wonders, going to the moon, satellites beaming information around the world, heart transplants, computers that can talk, and yet no one has ever been able to make an ant!

Orville and Wilbur Wright invented the airplane, Charles Goodyear showed us how to make vulcanized rubber, James Watt invented the steam engine, and Edison created the light bulb. But no one has ever been able to make a simple little ant from scratch!

I better shut up or somebody will be getting a research grant of half a million dollars from the government on how to make ants. They have to spend your money somehow or else their budget gets cut, you know! A project like that would meet their requirements too, because there is no demand or need for it anywhere!

ANT WALLPAPER

Anyway, we did have ants at our house and they were everywhere! Kim got out the bug spray and glued them all to the ceiling. Then she went down to the store and bought some poison ant stakes to put around the outside of the house. They were to be inserted into the ground every six feet, but before you do that, the directions said to pour water over them, insert a small stick into the hole where the poison is and stir the poison solution. Apparently, that activated the poison.

Kim sat at the living room table as she mixed the ant stakes. She would pour water over each one and then mix it with a plastic tooth-pick. Just about the time she finished, the doorbell rang and Kim set the poison-covered toothpick on the floor as she went to answer the door.

TOOTHPICKS CAN
STUNT YOUR GROWTH

Some people have the bad habit of smoking cigarettes, and some people have the bad habit of drinking too much alcohol. I happen to have the bad habit of sucking on tooth-picks.

Naturally, when I saw this attractive-looking, yellow plastic toothpick lying lost on the floor, I picked it up and put it into my mouth. I re-

"Orville and Wilbur Wright were rhinos!"

member thinking how sweet-tasting it was as I played with it between my teeth. After the sweetness had disappeared the toothpick lost its appeal however, and I discarded it.

Meanwhile, Kim had gone back to her job of activating the ant poison but couldn't find her toothpick. She immediately questioned me about it, and I told her that I had thrown it away.

Then with a look of sheer terror on her face, she asked me, "You didn't put it in your mouth, did you?"

WANNA BUY A TICKET TO ALASKA?

Aauugh!! The next ten minutes, Kim and I were frantically running around looking for the ant stake box to read the caution label. Oh no! The caution label was a danger label listing all those long, chemical names like you read on the side of cereal boxes! Arsenic was the main ingredient, and I knew that wasn't in there to provide for 100% of my minimum daily requirements.

O.K. Stay Calm. Don't panic. I quickly called the general hospital and told them what had happened and asked what they would suggest. They told me to come down immediately to the emergency room.

Oh no! Panic! I didn't want to hear that! Why couldn't they have just suggested drinking some orange juice or taking a hot bath?

On our way down to the hospital, as Kim was quietly sobbing, I could feel the poison starting to take effect. Was my breathing starting to get tight? Did my heart feel like it was starting to beat irregularly? Did I have a fever?

Then when I realized that I was probably dying, my mind raced over all that I had left undone. We were scheduled to go to Alaska in two weeks. Would Kim go by herself? Could she get our money back on my unused ticket? How was Kim going to know that the car was due to go in for its 12,000 mile check next week?

DYING OF EMBARRASSMENT

We walked into the emergency ward and they were waiting for us. The nurse said that she was expecting someone a little younger. What an embarrassing way to die! Why couldn't God have found a more noble way to bring me to Him?

As the nurse took my blood pressure, I showed the doctor the box listing all the poison ingredients and explained what happened. As I related the story, I wondered what he would do with me. Would he hook me up to a stomach-pumping machine? Would he give me some sort of injection? Or would he put me in the intensive care ward?

He did none of those things. After I told him the story . . . he *laughed!* He asked me if it was sweet, and I told him that it was, and that I could understand why the ants liked it. Apparently, I would have to take the amount that I did ten times a day for twenty years in order for it to have any adverse effect on me.

THANK YOU, LORD!

So, I got the car in for its 12,000 mile check, and we went to Alaska and had a fabulous time. I wanted to finish the book up with this story because it has a moral to live by as you are out charging through the jungle. That moral is:

A.) Don't try to commit suicide with poison ant stakes.
B.) Never leave the rind behind.
C.) Don't put toothpicks that you find on the floor in your mouth.
D.) Appreciate what you have and love life, because you never know when your time will be up.

MAY THE LORD ALWAYS GUIDE YOU ON ALL YOUR SAFARIS!

"Appreciate what you have and love life."

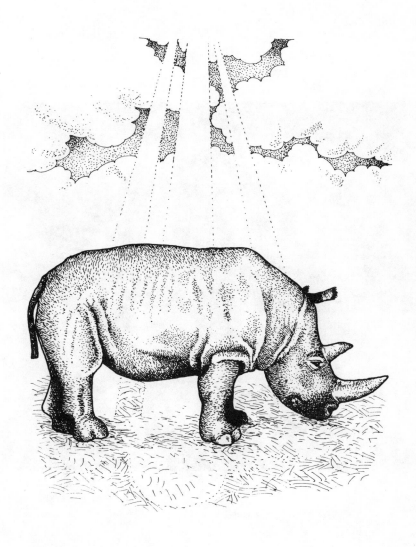

ABOUT THE AUTHOR

Scott Alexander and his wife, Kimber, were photographed here deep in the Southern California jungles.

Scott enjoys pizza with two-inch-thick crust, and being unemployable.

ABOUT THE ILLUSTRATOR

Laurie Smallwood is a freelance artist who lives in San Diego, California with her husband and son. Laurie loves the beach, animals, drawing and painting.

HAVE YOU READ "RHINOCEROS SUCCESS" AND "ADVANCED RHINOCEROLOGY?"

Scott's other two books, "Rhinoceros Success" and "Advanced Rhinocerology" are available directly from The Rhino's Press, Inc. for $5.95 ea. (That includes tax and postage.) We would love to send you a copy of each! And of course, if you would like additional copies of "Rhinocerotic Relativity" you may also order them directly from us for $5.95 ea. (tax and postage included)

We also offer quantity discounts of all three books with bulk purchase for educational, business or sales promotion use.

Send your order or request for more information to:

The Rhino's Press, Inc.
P.O. Box 2413
Laguna Hills, CA 92653
Ph. (714) 997-3217